The Business Side of SEO

Building a Business Within the Digital Marketing Industry

By Mark A Preston

Contents

Introduction

Why I'm Writing This Book

My main reason for writing this book is to educate the SEO industry. As a professional SEO trainer & speaker, I'm happily sharing my own experience of how I have tested nearly every method to sell SEO and what has worked well. This means you don't have to waste the thousands of pounds I have done in testing selling techniques that have just not worked.

I'm also very active in discussing the ethics of SEO. I speak at digital conferences throughout the UK, educating both business owners and digital marketing professionals on what ethical SEO is and how digital marketing agencies should approach ethics with their clients.

The problem in our great industry is that many SEO professionals and digital agencies make sales mistakes and create potential conflicts as they just don't know any different. I'm on a personal mission to make a difference and build some trust back into the SEO industry. If by reading this book it makes you think a little differently in your approach to your own sales process, as well as helping you to retain more clients, I have done what I set out to do.

My Own Journey

When setting up my first digital marketing business back in 2001, I always had a personal goal of building a business with zero investment and loans. To this day, I have never borrowed a penny from anyone and have always self-grown six figure businesses. Sure, I've had many ups and downs along the way and if I could turn the clock back, I would do a lot of things differently for sure.

One thing I did understand was that I couldn't just directly compete with the big players who had deep pockets to take on large teams of sales people on large salaries. I had to come up with an alternative way to grow and so I focused my efforts on getting other people to sell for me who I did not have to pay a salary to.

This is when I decided to split my business into two parts:

1.   I would provide a direct marketing service to businesses who would refer me to others. There is no better sales person than one of your own customers, so if you do a great job and have a fantastic relationship with your clients, they will do all the selling for you. It got to a point where I would pick the phone up and be greeted by – "Hi Mark, It's Paul here from Paul's Commercials. I was talking to John from John's Recruitment and he was telling me what a great job you've done and how well his business is doing. Can we set up a meeting to discuss how you can help me and when you can start?" I got myself into a position where people were willing to pay a premium to work with me.

2.   The second part of my business was the decision to go into the white label industry. I realised that there was a big problem in the industry; agencies needed extra resources to help them out but the only solutions on a white label basis were off-shore companies. I had worked out that by having zero sales costs, I could provide a great white label service at a reasonable price so agencies were still able to make a decent profit margin. I now had my competitors selling my services for me. OK, it was not under my own brand but it still ensured I could scale without any sales costs.

Using these two approaches, I would very easily and quickly grow my businesses to between £100K and £250K but found that a whole new set of issues sprung up once I reached this level.

Over the years, I've gone through two big recessions and come across almost every industry related issue imaginable. Writing this book is my way of helping you so you have a half-decent chance of making it work. If I can at least stop you from making some of the very costly mistakes I have made along the way, it will be worth it.

I'm not a millionaire and openly admit that I'm not even the best businessperson in the world. I'm just a regular guy who really understands the SEO and digital marketing industry, who has gone to hell and back at times and who just wants to make a difference.

Research For This Book
This book started one day as a tweet which grew into an article then eventually became this very book you are reading now.

Now, I want to make one thing perfectly clear right from the start. This book is meant to be a guide. It is an overview of my own experiences and what has proven to be successful for me over the years. How much of this book you will implement will depend on how you have structured your own agency. If nothing else, it will provide some great useful information and a solid actionable process you can at least think about.

Feedback I Received

Like anything I write, no matter if it is a news piece for my local newspaper, an article for one of the major online marketing publications or a book, I only write topics that people actually want to read and that there is a real need for.

This book is based on a subject that has not been written over and over again, as digital marketing agencies do not want anyone to know how they secure and convert their leads. However, if I went ahead and started writing this book based on my own individual thoughts without reaching out to others and asking them what they want to know, this book would not be successful.

During my guide and book research, I have been talking to SEO professionals and agency business owners to ask them if they would find a book about selling SEO and retaining clients useful, if I created one. A massive 93% of all people I reached out to said that it would be a fantastic idea.

I wanted to go one step further and ask my connections what related subject matters they'd like me to tackle by listing down the questions they had. I received loads of fantastic feedback and below are the common ones that cropped up multiple times:

- How do you find prospects?

- How do you present SEO services?

- How do you close the deal?

- What have you tried that doesn't work?

- How do you calculate the ROI?

- What are the different revenue models?

- How much should I charge?

- How do you first approach a new prospect?

- How do you work out the price of SEO packages?

- How do you find people who value SEO enough to pay your prices?

- How do you educate people so they do value it?

- How do you set the right expectations?

- What reaction do you get from a prospect?

- How do I put a contract together?

I am going to try and cover all the above questions within this book, amongst others, but I also need to make sure that the information is universal so that any SEO freelancer or large agency, in any Country, can follow the steps I have documented.

I know that there is a real need for this book and I am perfectly placed with no conflict of interest, to be the one who writes it.

A message from Nikolay Stoyanov of the White Hat SEO group on Facebook

This group is where I performed a large part of my research.

"Mark Preston is one of the most experienced, respected and friendly SEO experts I've ever met.

Here's the short story of how we met and what inspired him to write his book.

I created a white hat SEO community on Facebook in 2016 and one day Mark Preston asked to join. We quickly started communication within the community, discussing interesting SEO topics daily. We soon became friends and moved our discussions to Skype. Since we met we've spent countless hours exchanging opinions on various SEO subjects.

In the Facebook 'White Hat SEO – Learn It Now' group, I try to help all members with their daily SEO struggles and to make them realise that the future belongs to ethical SEO. I guess I can be considered a white hat ambassador in a way.

As time went by, my group members started asking more and more questions related to client acquisition. Many of them are SEO professionals – either freelancers or company owners. They all had the same problem. They didn't know how to get more customers.

One day, during one of our discussions, I asked Mark for his professional help with this subject. He has over 15 years of experience in our industry and I was sure he'd be able to help. And so, he did!

Mark created a poll within the group which quickly became one of the most engaging posts in the community ever. He asked all members one simple question: "Do you want me to write a very detailed, step-by-step guide on how to generate more SEO leads and sales? If so, what would you like to know?" People were very excited, so he began writing it!

Within a couple of weeks, the guide was finished and Mark shared it in the white hat group. Everybody was thrilled and thankful! I can safely say that today his guide turned into a reference book for everyone who wants to acquire more quality SEO leads and sales.

I can certainly say that Mark Preston is one of the most experienced and friendly SEO experts I've ever met in my career.

I find his SEO Sales Guide probably the ONLY piece of content that covers the topic of acquiring new SEO clients on the Internet. It's very thorough, easy to comprehend, highly actionable and easy to execute.

I am looking forward to reading his book on the topic and am honoured to have become one of the reasons Mark decided to write this future bestseller".

With huge respect, Nikolay Stoyanov.

My Fair Share of Mistakes Along the Way

I did say that I have wasted thousands of pounds on sales, marketing and lead generation ideas that have fallen flat. Here are just a handful.

Selling services, I cannot do personally

When it comes to SEO, I like to think of myself as an expert but when it comes to graphics, infographics and general design, I'm totally useless. When you are sat in front of a potential client, you need to be able to answer any question at all without even having to think about it.

Buying SEO leads

I have spent many thousands testing all kinds of SEO lead providers on all pricing levels and although I did manage to convert some leads, I made a total loss. The reason being that these leads are sold to many different people, so when you pick up the phone to discuss their requirements, they have been totally hounded and you often get a response like: "I've had loads of calls and don't have a clue who anyone is". Remember that they did not request a quote from YOU or your agency.

Trying to be everything to everyone

A few years back, I was just like most of you who think their client is anyone and everyone. My own thinking was that I could offer something to anyone, no matter how much or how little they had. I tried to capture the whole market, from your low-cost start-up businesses to blue chip brands. What I actually ended up doing was creating one massive mixed message sales funnel. In fact, the funnel was not even populated as nobody was enquiring due to the indifferent sales copy.

Purchasing email data to send sales emails

I very quickly learned that unless you are willing to pay a hefty price for a top-quality email database, you soon get blacklisted. I even tried to use a third-party email that was not lined to my domain but because the body of the email contained my website URL, my domain still got blacklisted and I just could not get myself removed. You can imagine the issues I had trying to communicate via email. Now, unless it is an email list of my own that someone has double opted into to receive information from ME, I just don't do bulk sales emails.

Advertising in the totally wrong places

You name it, I've tested it when it comes to paying for advertising. Magazines, newspapers, Yellow Pages, banner adverts, the list goes on. The problem was that they were just not targeted, or were targeted at totally the wrong audience. I spent a lot of money each month advertising in top web design magazines, as I thought that people who read those magazines would also need SEO services. Totally the wrong thinking. I learned the hard way that you should always advertise where your ideal client is and do thorough research before spending anything.

SEO Marketing and Pre-Sales Process

It does not matter what industry you are in or what product or service you sell, it is important that you document a marketing and sales process. Why? Because without a process to follow, you are just stumbling along day after day in the hope that the phone is magically going to ring.

I've seen it so many times; business owners just expect the phone to ring because they are good at what they do. The phone will never ring unless you do something to make it ring.

Sales and marketing is all about doing something regularly. This regular activity will then start to fill your sales funnel and turn into new business. In this book, I am going to go through the exact selling process I have used for years to confirm small contracts worth £500 per month and high profile seven figure contracts with established brands. The process is the same, the only thing that changes is the audience you target.

Many people over complicate lead generation and sales but I tend to simplify everything I do. Generating sales is just knowing who you want to target, finding where they hang out, building relationships with them and then pushing that piece of content that converts them.

A typical sales cycle looks like:

Selling SEO is no different from selling anything else. If you have the solution to match a customer's pain points and you can prove that you are THE only agency to deal with – job done. It's all about the Know – Like - Trust – Buy factor.

- For someone to buy something from you they have got to trust you.

- For them to trust you they have got to like you.

- For them to like you they have got to know you.

This is the perfect lead generation and sales cycle. Keep this in mind when you create and implement your own sales process.

What Are Your Own Business Goals?
I am contacted on a weekly basis from digital marketing professionals who have handed in their notice to go it alone as a freelancer. Whilst many ask me questions related to certain SEO techniques, a lot

of questions are related to the business side of running and building a successful SEO or digital marketing industry.

One of the first things I ask is - what are your own business goals? It surprises me that these people are marketing professionals but have not even considered their own business goals.

It is so important that you fully understand what your realistic business goals are because this is the solid foundation for all your sales.

It's just like when you write a business plan; you always start at the end and work backwards. If your goal is to sell the business in five years' time for £3m, you need to start working backwards to demonstrate how this will be achieved and the level of sales and revenue you will require.

If your own business goal is to give up your nine to five job and earn a decent living by working for yourself, your sales plan is going to be dramatically different to someone who has £1m to invest in starting up a full-service digital marketing agency with multiple offices around the world within five years.

It is also very important to be realistic when putting together your business goals. Over the years, I have had to turn around and tell so many businesses and companies that their business goals and objectives are never going to be met because they are totally unrealistic. Many people have this mind-set of thinking that because they're good, the sales will come in.

What Do I Sell – Time or Packages?

Let's discuss revenue models. There are not actually that many revenue model options when it comes to SEO. The options available are:

- Price per set package / service (one-off)

- Price per set package / service (monthly)

- Price per hour

- Set day rate

- Total price per campaign

- Monthly campaign price

These are the most common SEO revenue models that freelancers and agencies follow. Before you decide on which revenue model you wish to follow, there are a few questions you need to ask yourself:

• How large do you want to grow? Personally, I'm quite happy just being me. I have no interest at all in building a large agency. I've already done that and never want to do it again as I have finally found the perfect work / family balance.

• Do you need to employ people? If so, can you recruit staff quickly and easily? The digital marketing industry is growing at such a rapid rate, you only have to look on LinkedIn to see that agencies all over the world are crying out for skilled marketing staff. Usually it is the large agencies with the fancy offices and deep pockets that bag all the best staff. One agency I went in recently had a full games room and a slide in the centre it. Just because you have a job opening does not mean marketers will be flocking to come and work for you because reality is – there are just not enough marketers within the industry to cope with rapid demand.

• If you are considering outsourcing the work, do you have a top-quality outsourcing team who are reliable, trustworthy and perform every task ethically?

It does not matter how much research you have done, the fact is that if you outsource your client's work, you lose a certain level of control. On the other hand, if you have found a very good outsourcing partner who knows their stuff and communicates perfectly, you are going to have to pay good money for them. You then have to look at your profit margins; there is no point at all in running a business if you are not making any profit.

• Do you have the personal skills to complete any task? If you are let down by an outsourcing provider or a member of staff calls in sick just as a deadline hits, you need to have the skills to personally complete any task yourself so that your client is never let down. Staffing issues have to be the vein of every single business owner. It does not matter how good your staff are, they will never be as dedicated and passionate as you are because it's not their business. There have been many times where a member of my team has called in sick at a very crucial point in the campaign and timing could not have been any worse. The client has everything in place for this massive promotional campaign based on a strict date and there are bits on your side that need to be completed. The member of staff who has called in sick is the only person that can complete that job. Basically, you are screwed. Having the personal knowledge and experience to complete any task if required will save your bacon many times.

• Do you have a ceiling capacity? How many clients do you need before you are at full capacity or need to expand your team? It does not matter what revenue model you go for, there will always be a capacity level that you cannot go above with your existing resources. Never take work on that you cannot fulfil or you will get yourself into one big legal mess and gain a reputation as a rip-off shark.

• Do you have the finances to maintain your team's salaries if you lose clients? It is hard enough to find decent staff in this industry, so the last thing you want to do is get a 'hire and fire' name for yourself. There are a lot of agencies who go through the vicious circle of securing new contracts – taking on staff to service those contracts – losing contracts for any number of reasons – having to lay staff off because there is not enough revenue coming into the business to pay them – replenishing those lost contracts –

having to find new staff to service those contracts. This scenario happens more often than you think. The main reasons are that either the agency is just not charging enough, so there is no surplus money in the bank to cover any downturns or they are simply spending money they don't have. Don't take staff on and promise them a long-term career if you cannot look after them. Besides, if you are seen as a 'hire and fire' agency, nobody will want to come and work for you and the marketers who do agree will have low morale.

- What is you out? By this I mean: what does your business plan look like? Are you considering selling up within five years and need to generate a certain amount of annual profit to make that happen, or do you just want to make enough money to have a comfortable life with no hassle, securing that ideal work / life balance?

Your answers to the above questions will determine which revenue model works best for you. If you go down the one-off sales route, you will always be chasing that next order. If, however, you go down the route of building up a residual income, the pressure of generating a constant flow of sales is not as great.

I would always suggest that you make sure your revenue model is based on building a good client base that pays you (on time) an agreed amount of money each month and stays with you long term. To achieve this though, you need to be damn good at what you do; over deliver on expectations, ensure the client's business goals are at least met and provide a fantastic customer experience.

How Much Should You Charge?

If a director of a company randomly selected ten different SEO agencies to provide a quote, I guarantee that they would receive a total mixture of quotes. I have had conversations with prospects who have told me that they are in the process of requesting quotes which have been between £200 per month, right up to £10,000 per month.

So how much should you charge?

This is the million-dollar question that every SEO based business wants to know. As far as I am aware, the most common ways SEOs determine their prices are:

Based on Packages

The reason so many lower level SEO and digital marketing agencies stick to selling set packages is because it's easy. They simply put together three set packages, work out all the expenses, add a set percentage profit margin and hey presto; you have three separate priced packages for your prospective clients to choose from. Many think that this is a good way to go, as each client selects a package that matches their price point. As far as you are concerned, the client has received what they have paid for so there will never be any issues.

This is all well and good in theory but SEO or digital marketing in general is just not a one-package-fits-all world. Every single website and every single business is different in some way. Two people who purchase the exact same package may have totally different expectations.

On the plus side however, clients do want to fully understand what they are getting for their money.

Based on Time

Most large agencies charge by time (usually per day based on man hours) as they are able to grow based on a time model. Their hourly rate is usually determined by what their competitors are charging, as well as taking into consideration all their business and staffing costs.

This works out well for a lot of agencies as they are just selling their time. They know that each member of staff can work xxx hours per month that they can sell. Once all members of staff have reached their time limit, they must increase staffing levels. So long as you can maintain your existing client base, it is a good way of scaling your business.

There is however a problem with this. If clients are paying for time, they often start to think about how much they could save by taking a professional marketer on in-house to do basically the same work. It is your job to demonstrate true value as a great alternative.

Unlike paying for a set package, many prospects are wary about paying for time as they just do not understand what they are getting for their money. Simply saying that you will work on their campaign for 40 hours per month at a cost of £3K is just not good enough. You need to demonstrate what you are going to do within those 40 hours.

Based on Campaign

Some agencies provide a set campaign price based on a set period of time. How they actually come up with that price is anyone's guess. Most just pluck a figure out of thin air whilst the minority strategically base the price on estimated time, campaign expenses, staff wages and profit margins.

Personally, I would put a proposal together with a price based on the campaign which demonstrates how the client's goals and expectations will be met over a set period of time. This will be focused on return on investment.

Let's say that the client's goals were to increase their revenue by £200K over the next 12 months. I usually work on a 10% investment level so that you have around £20K over the 12 months to make this happen. You can then split this down into quarterly instalments based on achieving progressive targets.

As this is a guide that any level of SEO freelancer or agency can follow in any country, I'm not going to tell you how much you should charge, as prices dramatically vary and are determined by so many different criteria.

I don't mind telling you what I charge. As a high-level professional SEO trainer & speaker and the person who train the award-winning marketing teams, my fee starts at £995 per day. I do also charge travel and accommodation expenses on top of this.

Personally, in my own business, I have very little expenses and no staff. In order to scale my business, I would have to find a digital marketing expert who has the same level of knowledge and experience as myself, has been in the industry for over two decades, is totally passionate about what they do and just loves the industry. Oh yes - and someone who can stand in front of professional marketers working within global companies and deliver a confident training session. If you know of such a person, please do give them my contact details! But seriously, for me, I have to be realistic and understand what my own capacity is. After all, there is only me and I only have so many days in a month that I can sell. This means my income potential has a ceiling capacity that I have to be happy with.

I have set my own pricing structure based on value for money and at a price that companies and agencies will pay for multiple times. You need to set your own prices according to the value that YOU have to offer without pricing yourself out of the market.

If I were to look at what digital marketing agencies charge here in the UK, their rate would average at £320 to £750 per day, depending on location and the size of the agency. So, if you are pitching to a company based in the centre of London, they might not entertain a proposal priced at £320 per day because it is seen as having no value. Being the cheapest often works against you.

The best rule of thumb for setting your prices

The best piece of advice I can give you for establishing what you should charge is to do your research. List down all the SEO agencies and freelancers that service your target demographic client. Get a friend with a business that matches your ideal customer demographics and get them to contact all your competitors for a quote. Drain as much information as you can from them. Things like pricing and what they provide for that price are a good start.

It is so important that you do this because this is exactly what your potential customers will do. Knowing what your competitors are telling your prospects is very valuable.

List down each agency. Note how long it took for each one to reply, their price / quote, pricing structure and everything they provide within that price. Once you have all this information, you can put together your own pricing structure that provides a lot better value for money than all your competitors. You do however still need to make a profit. Makes perfect sense, right?

Set Priced SEO Packages

I was asked by a lot of SEOs about pricing set SEO packages. I have provided white label SEO packages to agencies throughout the world for over ten years and found that the only way white label works is for me to provide set priced SEO packages. It's not a strategy I would normally suggest for anyone selling direct to companies, as what works for one business may not work for another.

When you put a package together, it needs to totally relate to your 'must have' client. Do not confuse them by offering ten packages. Keep it simple and to the point with only three packages. I offered just three packages myself: 'Local SEO Package', 'National SEO Package' and 'Ecommerce SEO Package'. This way prospects just selected the package that matched their business.

I'm not going to go into what you should include within each package as you need to decide that based on your own skills, capabilities and resources. Don't put any numbers against anything and just list all the various tasks with a tick. You then put a 'from' price against each package. That way you are not seen as too cheap, plus you then have the option up-sell if a prospect has a higher budget.

There is no right or wrong when it comes to pricing. As long as your prices fall in line with what the majority of your demographic clients are willing to pay, that's a good start. You do however have to think about your client. They are purchasing one of your SEO packages because they need to generate more leads and sales. If your package does not provide a return, they will soon cancel.

To Contract or Not to Contract?

It does not matter how you structure your business. It does not matter if you provide SEO services or set packages. It does not even matter if you charge a one-off fee or have a residual payment structure.

Always Get it in Writing

Whatever you have agreed with your new client, draft a document that states exactly what you have both agreed and any terms associated. Both parties need to sign it. If it is not in writing, you don't have a leg to stand on and you open yourself up to all kinds of potential disputes. All you are doing is protecting both parties so that both you and your new client fully understand what needs to happen and when.

I talk to a lot of SEO agencies (mainly smaller ones) who don't do contracts or any kind of signed documentation as it slows the whole sales process down. It really does not have to. I use DocuSign for all my business documents and contracts. It's so easy to set up and you can tell if a prospect has read the document and when they have signed it. If I see that they have read it but not signed it, I simply give them a call and ask them if there is anything wrong with the agreement I sent them.

As legal documents and contracts differ from country to country and from time to time, I'm not going to provide a sample contract template. It is highly advisable to just pay a local solicitor or lawyer to draft up a sample SEO contract template. This template will be based on your own business and payment terms and will also match your offerings.

Without a contract, you cannot scale and grow your business

One of the biggest mistakes I have made when growing agencies is not getting my clients to sign some form of a contract. I had a belief that clients were going to stay with me long term because I do a great job. Slap me around the head with a big fish. How wrong was I?

Yes, I did provide an exceptional level of service. Sure, things did go wrong from time to time but I always put a solution in place. It was because I never asked any client to sign a contract that I found them cancelling for all sorts of reasons. Some being:

- Thanks for getting me to the top. I don't need you anymore.

- I've over spent and need to cut back on expenses for a couple of months.

- I was talking to a mate at the 19th hole who said he could sort this out for me.

- It's been two weeks and haven't seen any results.

Whatever the reason, if it is not in writing, you will be chasing your tail all the time and there will be lots of peaks and dips within your monthly revenue along the way, instead of building a gradual incline.

Your Audience

Not Everyone is Your Client

One of the biggest issues I find when talking to some SEO agencies is that they don't have a clue who their customers are. There does not seem to be a focus on any certain demographic. When I ask them "Who is your ideal customer?" I usually get a reply that goes something like; "Anyone with a website". No, no, no and no again.

If you sell low price set SEO packages on your website, you will only attract a certain demographic such as start-up businesses with very little money to invest. Then your business model becomes 'price low and high volume' or as I call it 'busy fools'. If, however, you want to build a brand that works with established companies who have a few thousand per month to invest, you are immediately turning away a certain demographic.

You can't be everything to everyone so decide on a certain demographic audience to target and brand yourself and your website according to their needs.

I tried to target both ends of the demographic scale at the same time and it just did not work. On one hand, there were established companies who would not entertain me because I sold set packages and on the other hand, my sales message was talking to a different audience.

By deciding on a certain demographic, you have a fighting chance to grow your business and make it work. Sure, you are effectively turning business away but at least you have a focus. Have you ever looked at a digital marketing agency's site that has large brands splashed all over the portfolio and also sells £200 per month set packages? No, you don't because it just does not work.

Deciding on a Target Demographic

Before we go any further, I want you to answer the following questions about who your ideal client is. Until you have a solid answer to each question, do not continue. It's not going to be easy for most of you but it is an essential part of the whole lead generation and SEO sales process. I suggest you base your answers on your own key strengths. If there is a certain area of SEO you specialise in then match that with your client demographics. There is nothing worse than being in a sales call or meeting and the prospect asks a question that you just cannot answer.

- What are your target industries?

- What are your target locations?

- What company size (number of employees) matches your ideal client?

- Who is the decision maker (the person who has the authority to sign your contract) within the company or business (director, marketing manager etc...)?

- What level of revenue / turnover do your ideal clients have?

- What are the similar business goals of your ideal target client?

- What are their pain points?

- What are the deciding criteria for a potential customer to convert into a paying client?

Did you find that hard? I did say it was not going to be easy but at least now you know exactly who your ideal target client is. That's half the battle!

If you are really struggling to get past this point, I suggest you list down all your own strengths and weaknesses within the SEO and digital marketing industry. Also, list down all your industry related achievements and results. Let's say that you have in-depth knowledge of how to drive local business through local SEO techniques but you have never actually ranked anyone for a national-based term.

This list will determine the path you go down and who you should be targeting. Focus on your own strengths; people are going to pay you as an expert in the marketing industry, so you need to be able to deliver.

It's OK to Have More Than One Target Demographic

As stated above, not everyone will be your target client but there are times in business when you might have the opportunity to target more than one specific demographic or you are expanding your range of services.

As an SEO trainer I have three target demographics myself:

1.   Established companies – I go into companies who have their own in-house marketing team to train them on how to put together a return-focused digital marketing strategy plan which is tailored to their specific business and industry. I will also train them on how to implement that plan. Additionally, I help many established companies who want to bring all their digital marketing in-house but don't really know how to.

2.   Digital marketing agencies - I am the person who goes into marketing agencies to up-skill professional marketers on the very latest updates and techniques that they can implement on multiple websites. I work in such a rapidly changing industry that nobody ever knows anything. I am only very good at what I do because I invest a lot of time into constantly researching, testing and keeping up with the very latest industry news. As most agencies are already stretched they cannot allocate research time for their staff. So, I go in on a regular basis to up-skill a group of professionals.

3.   Small business owners – These are businesses who do not have the budget to employ a digital marketing agency, as every penny counts. The problem is that they don't understand what to do either, so I host SEO workshop seminars throughout the UK where these small business owners can attend for a small fee to learn the basics.

Now, if you sit back and think about this for a minute: these are three very different demographics and it is important that I drive the right person to the correct page on my website.

How to Spot That High Value Client

Unless you have chosen to go down the cheap and cheerful route, you need to be able to spot the high value clients and the ones who will need an awful lot of work to turn a profit.

My stupid but simple rule of thumb is to look at the products or services they offer. You need to target the companies where their average customer is worth four figures. Think about it for a moment, if they generate an extra 20 sales per month and each sale averages £2,000, it means that (thanks to your SEO efforts) they will turn over an extra £40K per month in revenue.

Considering that an average business will invest around 10% of their revenue back into marketing, you can quite easily work towards charging £4K per month and the client would be happy to give it to you.

Let's turn this scenario on its head.

If you try to secure new clients where their average customer is worth £10 and you charge £1,000 per month, that business would need to secure 100 sales per month just to pay your fee and they would still be making a financial loss at that.

Content

Why is Content Important?

Many people mistake the word 'content' as sales text or blog posts but to me content is the backbone of any lead generation and sales process. Without content, you simply do not have a sales process.

From start to finish, all the way through your sales funnel, you are communicating to your potential client and every single form of that communication is content. If you say the wrong thing, it could mean the difference between winning or losing the contract.

Your content needs to relate to the person that is reading it. It needs to touch them emotionally. I'm not talking about them springing into floods of tears but instead making them truly believe that you fully understand their pain points. Crap like "you need to buy from us because we are very good" needs to stop, as nobody is falling for it anymore.

Does Your Website Sell?

Now that you understand who your ideal client is, you need to relate every page on your website to match their wants and needs. I see so many businesses publish sales copy on their website full of "look at me – aren't I just wonderful? WOW, I'm just super amazing".

Stop doing that shit. The truth is nobody cares about YOU. When someone lands on your website they only care about solving their own pain points and making sure that you or your agency is the one that can indeed solve their issues.

As a very brief outline, each page on your site must do three things:

1. Provide the solution to their problem

By this I mean, besides ensuring your content matches the search's intent, they have landed on that page because they have a certain problem. As an example, if you have a page relating to local SEO services, there is a high chance they need help to drive leads and sales within their geographical area.

NOTE: Customers do not care about rankings. They only care about driving new business forward. They have not come to you because you might be able to get them to the No.1 spot on Google. To them, SEO is just one of the possible marketing engines that enables them to secure more leads and sales.

Your content needs to be written in such a way that it totally relates to them and solves their problems.

2. It needs to build trust

You need to put yourself in a position where every prospect is in the mind-set that you are THE person or agency to deal with. Not just one possible agency out of many but THE one. You only get yourself into that position by building trust. You need solid proof that you can actually do what you say you can do.

For example, if the sales copy on your website states you WILL (not can) help them to drive new business on a national scale, you need to have solid proof to back this up - or at least state that proof will be provided upon request.

3. Call-to-action

This is so simple but so very underused. The fact is, you need to tell your potential customers (they are not just website visitors) exactly what you need them to do next. Whatever action you want them to take will completely depend on the purpose of the page. If you don't call to action, guess what's going to happen? The chances are nothing at all!

Lead Generation

For some reason, I have always found it easy to generate leads. To me it's just logical thinking! However, most agencies find it hard to generate a constant flow of inbound leads. The fact is, they have just not put together the right process. Somewhere along their sales process there is a brick wall that needs to be knocked down before the flow of leads can happen.

Think of it this way; you are more likely to make the sale if someone comes to you with a problem that you can solve rather than to drag them kicking and screaming to your website when they have no interest in what you provide, or worse still – they have no need for your service. Makes perfect sense, doesn't it?

ALWAYS think targeted! From doing the exercise I laid out earlier in this book, you now fully understand what the demographics of your target clients are. Now stop wasting your time doing things that will never attract your ideal client!

The Perfect Lead

The perfect SEO lead is when prospects have contacted you. This may be through your website, via email, telephone or through one of your social media profiles. Your main focus must be to get them to contact you before you contact them.

I receive leads every day and am in a fortunate position where I can pick and choose who I want to work with. Yes, I do turn business away if it is not the right fit for me. This is the position you need to be in.

The No.1 Rule of Selling SEO

The number one rule of selling SEO services is to make sure your own website is ranking high for search phrases that your target demographic is likely to use. If you are offering local SEO based services then you need to make sure you are ranking high locally in both the maps and organic search. If you are offering national based SEO services you need to make sure that you are ranking on a national scale for your target search phrases.

Paid Adverts

I have a pure love for SEO but always advise anyone, no matter what industry they are in, to run a paid campaign.

When you mention paid campaigns to anyone the first thing they think about is Google AdWords. They go ahead and setup a pay per click campaign on AdWords and invest all their paid budget into this one platform.

There are many opportunities outside of Google to setup and run a great paid advertising campaign. Split your advertising up to capture as many people as possible. I have said this before; advertise where your potential customers hang out. If you spend £1,000 placing an advert on a top SEO news site, guess what? You will attract other SEO professionals.

Before you invest the time and effort into any other form of lead generation, you need to run a paid campaign for a full month. This will provide you with fantastic data and allow you to determine whether or not the content on your website converts. If the paid campaign is not generating leads, you need to find out why and rectify the problem. Usually it is because you are not building any trust and your content does not relate to the reader.

If your PPC campaign is driving quality leads, you are in a fantastic position to push your other lead generation methods.

Organic Leads
I'm reading and hearing a lot of so-called digital marketing industry experts going around saying that a good SEO agency does not need their own site to rank high. Bullshit! Prospects need to feel confident that your agency can secure results and 85% will still base things on your own site ranking high.

Over the years, I have established that there are four top money keywords that companies use when they have already established that they need SEO and are looking for an agency or individual to make it happen. If you can secure top rankings for even one of these phrases, leads will start to flow in. Also, make sure you are ranking for the related local terms as well.

If you are an agency with a team behind you, ranking high organically for these phrases will drive a constant flow of quality leads:

- SEO Agency / SEO Agencies

- SEO Company / SEO Companies

- SEO Services

- SEO UK (or your own country)

If you are a freelancer your money keywords are:

- Freelance SEO Consultant

- SEO Expert

- SEO Consultant

- SEO Consultant [TOWN]

I have ranked high on the first page organically for quite a few of these phrases, so I fully understand the quality of leads they generate. I also found that the phrase 'SEO UK' is an untapped gold-mine that many agencies never go after. Ranking for this one (less competitive) phrase generated a lot of leads from international brands who are No.1 in their own country and who want to launch within the UK marketplace. These types of brands also have a great budget to invest.

Frankly, if you are not able to rank high organically for at least one of those phrases, maybe you should think about a different career.

Email Marketing

When I mention email marketing to people they tend to relate this to purchasing an email database of potential clients and sending them a cold email hoping that someone will reply.

I have news for you. The General Data Protection Regulation (GDPR) prevents you from doing this and if found out, you could be facing a massive fine. I would suggest that you seriously read up about the GDPR before sending another email to anyone to ensure you conform to laws.

A good example of the kind of spam emails that are being clamped down on go something like:

Hi,

I hope you are well. I was just looking at your website and despite it having a good design, I noticed it is not ranking anywhere....... blah, blah, blah....

I must receive hundreds of these shitty emails each month. If by any slim chance you are one of the people who are still sending these trash emails, besides going against the GDPR laws, let me explain what the recipient is thinking:

Hi, [HI WHO?]

I hope you are well. [NO YOU DON'T] I was just looking at your website [REALLY!] and despite it having a good design, I noticed it is not ranking anywhere [WHO GIVES A SHIT AND BESIDES, I'M RANKING AT THE TOP ALREADY] ……. blah, blah, blah…. [DELETE EMAIL NOW. I CAN'T READ ANYMORE].

The days of the 'blast it out and see what we can catch' attitude is long gone as a lead generation tactic. This email is just one example of the sort of crap that still happens. I can however give you tons of similar examples where you just chuck your brand in people's faces, whether they want to see it or not, in the hope that by some slim chance someone and anyone contacts you.

The correct way of performing email marketing is to build a list. Ever heard the saying 'the money is in your list'? This is basically a process of writing informational based content that provides massive value to the reader and entices them to subscribe (double opt-in) to your newsletter because they know you are going to send them further tips that will help them.

These people have stated they are happy to receive emails from you, so informing them about one of your services amongst providing something of value for free will usually generate quite a few leads.

Creating Your Prospect Database
If you are sat at your PC day after day with no inbound leads being received, you need to be proactive and go and reach out to potential prospects. Many SEOs struggle with this process, so I will explain how I would personally go about finding prospects and making that first approach.

Firstly, you need to have a targeted database of people and/or companies that match your target demographic client. Buying data is no longer an option and besides, it's never targeted.

I am going to explain a nifty hack which will allow you to generate any database you want with nothing more than two tools and a $15 investment.

You will need:

•   30-day free trial of LinkedIn Premium (Sales) or full Premium account

•   Professional addition of Dux-Soup ($15 per month)

Step 1 – Download the Dux-Soup Chrome extension and upgrade to the Professional version.

Step 2 – Login to your LinkedIn account. It is best if you have already re-written your profile and it is fully populated.

Step 3 – Go to the search feature on LinkedIn and using all the various search options, search for your target demographic.

If you have a Premium LinkedIn account, you can really narrow your search down to your exact demographic (company size etc..). They offer a 30-day free trial, so if you have not already taken advantage of the free trial then I would, as you will generate a much higher targeted database of prospects.

Step 4 – Whilst on the LinkedIn search results page click the Dux-Soup icon in the top right of your browser which will open a window with a few options. Click the 'VIEW PROFILES' button. The plugin will now automatically start to view each profile within the search results, notifying each prospect that you have viewed their profile. Did you know that 30% of those prospects will view your profile just because you have viewed theirs? This makes each prospect aware of who you are.

Step 5 – Click the 'DOWNLOAD DATA' button which will export a CSV file of all the profiles Dux-Soup has just visited.

Even though you are not connected with any of these people, the information you receive is gold dust. Considering you have only invested a mere $15 to get this information, it is crazy brilliant if you think about it.

- Name

- Job Title

- Company

- Personal LinkedIn Profile URL

- Company LinkedIn Profile URL

- Company Website

Any prospects you are already connected to on LinkedIn will output a lot more information.

Step 6 – As you are not connected with any of these people, their email and telephone data is hidden within the CSV. This is not a problem at all because the last thing you want to do is go ahead and spam them by sending unwanted sales emails.

This prospecting method has saved me many thousands of pounds in buying data. Please note: do NOT abuse this prospecting method, as LinkedIn filters will block your account.

Manually filter your prospect list

Now that you have your prospect list you need to go through it to make sure that each potential future client NEEDS your SEO services or packages. There is nothing worse than reaching out to a business and offering them SEO services only to find that their site is already at the top for all their targeted keywords and driving a ton of traffic.

Do your homework and research each company individually to create a concise list of the companies you can indeed help. It's quite simple. Just use one of the top SEO tools such as Ahrefs or SEMrush to determine what online visibility they already have.

Turning Your Prospect Database into Leads

I generate more high-quality leads through my LinkedIn profile than I do via my own website. In fact, I have generated £1m+ worth of business directly through LinkedIn over the past few years. If you are not working LinkedIn alongside your website as a lead generation tool, start now. It is a lead generation gold mine.

Don't try and sell directly through LinkedIn. Instead follow my example; I once posted an image on LinkedIn showing a screenshot of my top rankings along with a message that went something like, "I'm hearing a lot of chatter about local rankings bouncing around. Well I for one am loving the recent updates. It goes to show; ethical SEO always wins in the end."

Now that one post generated five red hot leads and I converted four into new SEO training clients, as it was solid proof that I knew exactly what I was talking about when it came to SEO. I think of it as indirect lead generation. You are just casting the bait waiting for someone to bite.

Never Spam LinkedIn

A massive mistake people do on LinkedIn, as well as other social platforms, is that they send a connection request and as soon as it has been accepted they send that person a sales pitch via private message. Not cool at all and it often results in you getting blocked by that connection.

You may gather from this book that LinkedIn plays a big part in generating those all-important leads. I cannot take all the credit for some of these LinkedIn lead generation techniques, as I learned them in one of Neil   Simpson's (https://www.linkedin.com/in/neilasimpson/) fantastic seminars.

If you can't make it to one of his seminars then take a look at my own LinkedIn profile (https://www.linkedin.com/in/markprestonseo/) to give you an idea of how to structure things. You won't go far wrong by following these six simple steps:

1.   Make sure you complete as much of your profile as possible.

2.   It is not your CV. Make sure you relate your summary to your target audience, making it crystal clear who you work with and how you can help them. Remember, it's about them and not you.

3.   Send a personal connection request to each one of your target prospects. Their LinkedIn URL is detailed within your prospect database.

4.   Work your feed to prove that you are an expert. Again, do not post sales messages. Provide value and educate.

5.   Keep an eye on the 'who's viewed your profile' and send them a personal message just saying something like, "Hi Mark, I noticed you was looking at my profile. Was there any specific reason?".

6.   Build relationships and get to a point where you are able to take the conversation offline. I always try to make a habit of arranging a call or Skype message with every one of my LinkedIn connections to move the conversation out of the virtual world.

This is a very basic step by step guide just to give you an idea but you will find your own process that works best for you. The most important thing with LinkedIn is consistency, doing something and doing it on a regular basis. Don't try it for a week and give up saying it did not work for you.

What to Do When a Prospect Connects

You have spent a lot of time and energy sourcing your target customer and they have connected with you. What now?

Now you must make that dreaded first approach. Something that sends shivers down grown men's spines and starts the blood pumping and the heart racing. Unless you already have a good inbound lead funnel, it is something you need to do.

Sending them an email to ask if they want a free website audit will just not cut it anymore. Start being a bit more creative and put yourself in their shoes. What would make you listen? Perhaps you can send them free gifts. This can basically be links to valued information that you have written. It needs to be something where, if they followed it, they could potentially increase new business. By doing this it builds trust - and you have not even tried to sell them anything.

Once you have their attention send them a short message through LinkedIn asking them if they have five minutes free during the next week for a quick call so that you can introduce yourself.

Research their company before the scheduled call and make the call all about them. During the conversation, get to know if they already work with a digital marketing or SEO agency. If so, is it working out for them?

That first conversation is a must without even trying to sell anything. It is a friendly chat in which you establish if there is an opportunity to do business or not. If they already work with another agency who they are happy with, cross them off your prospect list but keep in touch as you never know what will happen in the future. I have won lost business many times by sending a follow-up message via LinkedIn three months after I deleted them from my prospect list. A lot can happen in three months and in many cases you can step in to resolve their pain points at the exact time they need it. It pays to keep the relationship alive.

What if Prospects Just Do Not Connect?

You will find that not everyone on your prospect list will connect with you via LinkedIn. Don't be offended. I find that a lot of people only check their LinkedIn messages once per month. It might even be that they just don't accept connection requests from anyone they don't personally already know.

If this is the case I just bite the bullet and pick up the phone. Call them and ask them if it would be OK for you to post (yes, snail mail still exists) an introduction letter. The chances are they are going to say yes. Make sure you leave your name before you end the call and thank them.

Now you need to write a letter personally addressed to the decision maker (the person on your prospect list) describing how they would benefit from setting up a call or even a face to face meeting. Make sure you don't go overboard and keep it to one page. If you received a letter yourself, what would make you sit up and take notice?

Trust me when I say that this approach works a treat. It is just about starting a conversation and making each conversation about them.

The Selling Process

Squeezing a Budget Out of Prospects

So, you are at a stage where you have either received an enquiry or you are at a stage of talking business with a prospect you have warmed up.

I talk to agency directors on a daily basis and one big headache they have is the time and money they need to invest into the proposal stage with the hope that the prospect is going to confirm.

How many contracts have you lost because the proposal you presented was either too high or too low? I understand your pain because I've been there myself. The problem is that potential clients won't tell you if this is the case. They will just say that someone else was more suited.

The easy solution is to always get a budget.

Before you even think about writing a proposal, you need to squeeze a budget out of each prospect. I've lost count of the number of proposals I have written where the client has turned around afterwards and said that they have £100 per month to invest if they don't feed their kids but that £100 must turn a profit.

By getting a budget, you cut down on all the time you waste which allows you to focus on the prospects who do indeed have a realistic budget.

My own prospect to new client conversion rate has always been very good because I always got a budget that my potential clients were happy to invest. By getting a budget, it means that price will never ever be the reason for you losing the sale. Now that's a major step forward within the whole sales process.

I know exactly what you're thinking! I can hear it under your breath:

"But prospects never give me a budget, even if I ask for one."

I hear you and I have gone through the exact same thing myself. Therefore, over the years, I have been testing and tweaking different ways of dragging a budget from prospects. Here is usually how the conversation goes:

Me: "Yes, I can help you to increase new business but first I need to know what budget you have to make this work?"

Prospect: "I don't really have a set budget." OR "I just want a proposal so I can look it over."

Me: "The fact is, I have clients that pay me £500 per month and others that pay me £5,000 per month. The more they invest, the more effort we are able to put into their campaign, the more targeted traffic they will receive which all results in a higher return. There is just no point in putting a proposal together for you based on £4,000 per month if your marketing budget only stretches to £700 at most. This is just wasting both of our time. With this in mind, which end of the scale are you at?"

WAIT FOR THEM TO ANSWER

Prospect: "It's probably somewhere in between."

Me: "Thanks. So, if we put a proposal together based on £2,500 per month that demonstrated your estimated return on investment, would you seriously consider it?"

Prospect: "Yes, I would."

Me: "That's great news. In order for us to calculate an accurate return I just need to know what your average client is worth to you - in revenue terms that is. I also need to know what your lead-to-sales conversion rate is and what you need to happen to see this campaign as successful."

Prospect: "Well an average sale is worth around £1,500 and I convert about 20% of all leads into business."

Me: "And what sort of return would you need to receive to make this work for you?"

Prospect: "Around the £20K per month mark."

Me: "Fantastic. I don't see any reason we are not able to help you. Give me a couple of days to put a proposal together and I will give you a call once you have had time to go through it. I'm free either next Tuesday or Thursday. Which day is best for you?"

This conversation works for about 95% of all prospect calls I make. If for whatever reason they just will never give you a budget, you either must let them know that you are not able to move forward (which sometimes forces them into submission) or make a calculated guess.

How is Return on Investment Calculated?

If you can put together a proposal that demonstrates a solid return on investment, you are more likely to get your contract signed than if they receive a proposal that is just based on rankings and technical jargon.

I have a straightforward way of working out and documenting the potential ROI within a proposal and it goes like:

What we know

- Their average customer is worth £1,500.

- Their lead-to-sales conversion rate is 20%.

- They have stated that you need to increase revenue by £20K per month.

- Their accepted investment level to make this happen is £2,500 per month.

Over a six-month period, you need to generate 80 new customers to meet your target set above. [Calculation: monthly revenue times 6, divided by average customer amount]

We know that they convert around 20% of all leads they receive. In order to secure those 80 new customers, you need to generate 400 leads over the six-month period. [Calculation: 80 times 100, divided by 20]

A decent website realistically converts 5% to 10% of all targeted visitors into leads. If we use the lower percentage just to be on the safe side, we need to generate 8,000 visitors during the next six months. [Calculation: 400 times 100, divided by 5]. That averages out at around 44 visitors per day. [Calculation: 365 days per year. Half of that is about 182. Now divide 8,000 by 182]

That is how you work out the ROI for each prospect. Easy, wasn't it? Consider though that those 44 visitors per day are over a six-month period. It will take a while for you to start generating a constant flow of new visitors but when you actually split it right down, like in the example above, it sounds so much better than just sending a proposal stating, "we will increase your rankings for these five keywords and it will take six months."

How to Create a Winning Proposal

Over the years I have read hundreds of proposals from a wide range of agencies and to be truthful, most of them are just filled with waffle to beef the proposal up. The first five pages are all about the company and how great they are.

I just don't get it at all! You need to put yourself in your prospect's shoes. They don't need to be told how great your agency is - all that should have been discussed prior to them receiving a proposal. If you had not already built a certain amount of trust up, then they would not have accepted your proposal to be sent to them.

Keep the proposal short and sweet. You can even say to your potential client that you wanted to keep your proposal to the point instead of filling it up with fancy graphs that don't mean a whole lot. I've gained some respect by saying this as most directors are very busy people and don't want to go through a fifty-page proposal.

Apart from a personalised front cover, a proposal should include three things:

1.   The goals and objectives of the prospect.

2.   How you are going to achieve those goals.

3.   Your fees.

4.   The ROI, as demonstrated previously.

Directors or decision makers don't care if their site has loads of 404 errors or their mobile speed score is 40/100. What they care about is HOW you are going to help them increase new business. If you focus on what directors WANT to read then your lead to sales conversion rate will be a lot higher, as you are talking in their language.

I have even gone as far as asking prospects what they want me to document within their proposal. I get around this by saying that I don't believe in templated proposals and want to make sure they receive what they want. If nothing else, the director will remember you within a crowd.

Selling Face to Face

If possible, I always like to arrange a face to face meeting where I hand-deliver the proposal and talk through it. That way you can answer any questions they have straight away. This will put them at ease.

In fact, if it is a high value client, I even create a nice slide of the proposal and present it to the key decision makers within the company. I enjoy talking as I speak at quite a few expos and conferences, so presenting is no big deal for me. If you just don't have the confidence or your nerves start to go crazy at the thought of presenting, just stick to going through the paper copy only.

One big advantage of pitching live is that there is nowhere to hide. The prospect cannot just turn around and say, "I'll look at it next week" or "I'm busy right now".

I even go to a sales pitch with the contract already drawn up ready for them to sign. Some people think I'm daft for doing this and that you should always walk away and give the prospect time to think the proposal over.

The way I see it is that you have presented a proposal that is a no-brainer and you have answered every question the prospect has. So, what's there to think about? All you are doing is giving them time to change their mind.

If the proposal has been presented correctly, you won't have to do any selling.

Selling Over the Telephone

Over the years I have helped companies all over the world, so distance sometimes makes it impossible to present your proposal in person. You just need to make a decision on the value of the contract versus the expenses to meet face to face.

The second-best thing to presenting your proposal in person is to send it via post. Yes, snail mail again. I like to create a professional cover and bind the proposal between two sheets of plastic covers. You need to stand out and make your proposal as professional as possible. I also add a small gift within the package. Usually it is a small booklet on the top ten ways to drive traffic to your website for free.

The reason I do this is because it shows that I am a professional person to deal with and they have something tangible in their hands. They are never going to action any of the techniques in the booklet as they just do not have the time.

By now you will have built up a certain amount of trust and professionalism. Your proposal matches their investment level, they set it themselves so price is not an issue. The proposal is also written in a way that they can relate to with facts and figures.

There should be no reason at all why the prospect would disagree to your proposal. You do however need to set up an update meeting or call to discuss their thoughts on your proposal and whether they have any questions.

Once you have answered any questions they have, you need to get them to accept the proposal and sign your contract with an agreed start date and payment terms.

If at any time during this whole lead generation and sales process you have to SELL your services, you are doing something wrong. All I do is establish a need and present the solution.

If you need to twist their arm or bribe them into submission, you really do not want to work with those clients as you are only going to run into lots of problems during the campaign.

Selling via Email

For me this must be a last resort. Even low value prospects need to feel special, so investing about £5 in total to send a professional proposal by post (considering you will have a much higher conversion rate) is a no-brainer.

If for whatever reason you decide to email your proposal, make sure it looks very professional. Follow up by asking them if they received your proposal and if they have any questions.

Can you start to see why I don't use email to sell? It is very impersonal and cold but many agencies still use email simply because they fear picking the phone up and speaking to a real person. The fact is you are in business to make money so you need to get over your fears (and fast) or you might as well go and get a job.

But What if They Say No?

There will always be reasons beyond your control for lost sales. It happens to us all so there is no point crying about it.

The important thing is that you ask WHY you lost the sale.

Receiving feedback as to why you lost the sale is much more valuable than making the sale in some respects. No, I haven't lost my mind. If you don't know a problem exists then you can't fix it. If you never ask why you lost the deal, you will never increase your leads-to-sales conversion rate.

Over the years I have received fantastic feedback that I've used to tweak my sales process. All you need to do is ask the simple question; "It's disappointing that I was not given the opportunity to help you push your business forward but I appreciate that you have your reasons. Please could I ask why you decided against us working together?" I have never yet come across someone that would not tell me. In fact, it shows you care and if anything goes wrong with their existing setup, you will be the first person they call.

Getting Your Clients To Do The Selling

Happy clients are your best sales team
As you read at the beginning of this book, I have built my businesses over the years based on client referrals.

You simply have no better sales person than a happy client. I am a big believer that everyone knows someone and this is very true in business. Each one of your own clients also have their own clients and their clients have their own clients and so on... well, that is if you work with B2B clients.

By over-delivering on goals, targets and expectations along with constant and truthful communication, you have happy clients. Every client wants to feel as though they are the only client you have. Make them feel special and you are on to a winner.

Giving incentives for referrals
There are a lot of agency owners that really do not agree with me on this one. Giving clients an incentive to refer you to others is just not right, they tell me. A client should refer you to others because they want to and are happy to.

I however have a different mind-set. Would you ever recommend a company to a friend if you had received a bad service? Even if there is a financial incentive, you are just not going to refer your digital marketing agency to others if you are not totally happy with them yourself.

The way I explain it to happy clients is that I am providing them a way to receive the same level of service at a reduced price. I used to run a referral scheme where each client received 10% residual income for each referral who confirmed a contract. It did get to a stage where some clients were receiving a service at zero cost, as they had referred new business to us to ten times the value of their own contract.

If you do decide to introduce a similar referral scheme within your own agency, it is important that you only introduce this to your client when you are providing a great return. You must prove yourself before clients are happy to refer you.

References

People

Nikolay Stoyanov

Founder and Admin of 'White Hat SEO – Learn It Now' group

Twitter: @niksto82

White Hat SEO Facebook group:
https://www.facebook.com/groups/whseo/

Neil Simpson

LinkedIn Trainer

LinkedIn: https://www.linkedin.com/in/neilasimpson/

Author of LinkedIn Launchpad:
http://www.linkedinlaunchpad.com/

Research Tools

Ahrefs: https://ahrefs.com/

SEMrush: https://www.semrush.com/

Author bio

Mark A Preston is a very well-respected professional SEO trainer & speaker within the digital marketing industry. Armed with over two decades of industry knowledge and experience under his belt, he travels around the world training and educating marketing teams (both in-house and agency side) on the very latest ethical SEO and digital marketing techniques that help people to do their jobs better and give them a business development SEO mindset.

How to contact Mark A Preston

Website: https://www.markapreston.com

Email: me@markapreston.com

LinkedIn:
https://www.linkedin.com/in/markprestonseo/

Twitter: https://twitter.com/MarkPreston1969

Facebook:
https://www.facebook.com/markprestonseo

Thanks To My Publisher

For many years I've always wanted to write my own book. A few months ago, I connected with Matt Kinsella as he was on my top 100 list of influential business and marketing people, so we got talking. After a while, as Matt is a bestselling author himself, I mentioned that I always had an ambition to write and publish my own book but just had this idea that it would either be done badly if I did it myself, cost me thousands of pounds or I would end up doing all the work for a publisher to take the financial rewards.

How wrong was I. Matt offered me a book mentoring and publishing service that I snapped up. Whilst writing this book, I had many days where I just couldn't find the motivation to continue but during our weekly mentoring calls Matt always managed to give me inspiration to move forward and to recognise how easy it actually was. I can state 100% that if Matt had not been helping me through the process, my book would never have been finished.

Even before this book was released it directly boosted my credibility and authority in my field and led to better leads, clients and higher fees that I could charge.

Anyone can put out a self-published book or an eBook but Matt has helped me create a properly published book that is also marketed and promoted brilliantly.

As this book is about marketing and selling your services, I can recommend contacting Matt to help raise your business profile. I am already talking to Matt about writing my second book.

Everyone has a book in them and with the right help, it's not that hard. Just speak to Matt as he is a really friendly guy.

matt@mattkinsella.com

https://www.linkedin.com/in/matthewkinsella/

www.ingramcontent.com/pod-product-compliance
Lightning Source LLC
Chambersburg PA
CBHW071252170526
45165CB00003B/1317